CW00816262

UNICORN

UNICORN

THE POETRY OF

ANGELA CARTER

WITH AN ESSAY BY ROSEMARY HILL

P

PROFILE BOOKS

First published in Great Britain in 2015 by
PROFILE BOOKS LTD
3 Holford Yard
Bevin Way
London WC1X 9HD

www.profilebooks.com

Poems © Estate of Angela Carter, 2015
Essay © Rosemary Hill, 2015

1 3 5 7 9 10 8 6 4 2

Typeset in Quadraat by MacGuru Ltd
info@macguru.org.uk

Printed and bound in Great Britain by
Clays, Bungay, Suffolk

A CIP catalogue record for this book is
available from the British Library.

ISBN 978 1 78125 361 8
eISBN 978 1 78283 112 9

FSC
www.fsc.org
MIX
Paper from
responsible sources
FSC® C018072

In memoriam Christopher Logue 1926–2011

CONTENTS

PREFACE

This book has its origin in an essay written in 2012 for the *London Review of Books*. The occasion for it was Susannah Clapp's *Postcards from Angela Carter*, a short but evocative account of their friendship. The review gave me a chance to think again about Carter, an author who, like many of my contemporaries, I had not so much read as inhaled in the 1980s when I was in my twenties. Coming back to her, I found that, like one of her own creatures, she had grown and changed, becoming a more diverse and original writer than I had understood then – and harder to categorise.

When I wrote the piece my first husband, the poet Christopher Logue (1926–2011), had been dead only a few months. I was at that stage of loss when the dead still speak, not in a supernatural way (not to me at least) but because the conversation that was broken off is still fresh in the mind. It seems natural to ask them questions and to get answers. I could hear Christopher saying, as he had at times over the years: 'Angela Carter was very underrated as a poet.' I knew nothing of her poetry and could find nothing in print. What I did find, in Christopher's old school tuck box, where he kept books he especially valued and treasures like his letter from Ezra Pound, was a stapled, typed copy of 'Unicorn'. Much later, when this book was in progress I found among his papers a letter from 2000 which showed that he himself had tried and failed to get it reprinted.*

Reading 'Unicorn', I saw what he had admired. Here as if in bud were the themes that grew into the strange, extravagant, sometimes sinister blossoms of her later work. She and Christopher did not know each other, though they met once or twice in Bristol in the 1960s, when anyone might meet anyone. Yet when I came to think about their work together I saw parallels. 'Unicorn' takes a medieval myth and plays on it as Carter later played on themes from fairy tales. Christopher's best-known work was his reimagining of the Iliad, *War Music*. He described himself once as 'a rewrite man – like Shakespeare', and Carter, who used Shakespeare's

---

* This book is, to that extent, a tribute to him as well as to Carter.

plots when she wanted to, might have said the same. Both of them produced some of their best writing out of the constraints and opportunities offered by a pre-existing narrative. Both turned them into new works that were not only original but violent and sexualised in ways that have caused offence to those who would in general prefer to look away. In following Carter's trail of imagery I found her path crossed Christopher's more than once.

An historian's life is spent looking backwards and inevitably there comes a moment when, in the rear-view mirror as it were, you glimpse a familiar figure who is your younger self passing into history. Writing about Carter's work, I have found myself, reluctantly, a small part of the story. Not because I came to her poetry by way of Christopher's, nor because, in their historical context, I could see affinities between them as writers, but because, through Christopher, I had more first-hand knowledge of the literary world of the 1950s and 1960s than most of my contemporaries. I knew Austryn Wainhouse well. It seems astonishing that the first man to translate Sade in full into English died only in 2014. His versions were the ones Carter used for her most controversial book, *The Sadeian Woman*. They were a product of the post-war literary scene in Paris, which was significant as both background and influence in

Carter's early writing. I heard a lot about that scene from Christopher, who was also part of it, and from his friends from that time, John Marquand and George Plimpton, who founded *The Paris Review*. I knew the sad story of the pop artist Pauline Boty, and I knew her orphaned daughter. Nell Dunn, one of the most clear-eyed writers about women's experience in the 1960s, is a friend and she has been generous with her time in talking about the cultural climate of those days and the difficulties women writers faced.

Pondering the conventions of the critical essay, I decided to follow them so far as to call Carter and others I never knew by surnames, but that it would be odd and disingenuous to do the same with friends like Nell, or with Christopher. If there is a certain unevenness of tone as a result I can only say that it reflects my own semi-detached relationship with the subject matter and that such a half-in, half-out condition in relation to narrative is often found in Carter's work and so perhaps is not out of place in a discussion of it.

The part of the past that is most inaccessible at any given moment is the part where the 1960s are now: on the cusp of living memory. Too close to be seen in proportion, too distant to be remembered with accuracy, with too many documents still unpublished and too many vested interests among the living, it can only hover on the edge of the historian's peripheral vision. With this in mind I decided against publishing poems that survive only in manuscript. Carter clearly felt they were unfinished and I concluded that they therefore belong more properly to biography than anthology. It is possible that I have not found all of those she did publish and in that knowledge, and with my own, inevitable, preferences and areas of uncertainty set out, I have written about the poetry itself and about its place in the decade that produced it, which was not, as Carter once said, 'like the movies'. My essay is an expanded version of that earlier review and it serves as a tailpiece to the poems which are collected here for the first time to take their place in the oeuvre of a remarkable writer.

THE POEMS

Unicorn

Unicornis the unicorn. No hunter can catch him but he can
be trapped by the following stratagem. A virgin girl is led to
where he lurks and there is sent off by herself into the
wood. He soon leaps into her lap when he sees her and
hence he gets caught.

SIR THOMAS BROWNE

Let us cut out and assemble our pieces.

a) <u>The Unicorn</u>

       As with the night-scented stock, the full
splendour of the unicorn manifests itself most potently
at twilight. Then the horn sprouts, swells, blooms
in all its glory.   SEE THE HORN
                    (bend the tab, slit in slot
                    marked 'x')

SEE THE HORN SEE THE HORN SEE THE HORN

(running through ripping
the bulging belly of the dark)

Q. What have unicorns and virgins got in common?
A. They are both fabulous beasts.

b) <u>The young girl</u>

       She is all white and naked; arrange her
among innocent and fragile leaves, dripping
with last night's rain. A balloon comes
on a chain of bubbles
out of her head; she is comforting herself
with the pathetic fallacy, 'even
the trees weep for me
in my predicament.'

  She is raw and huge and her breasts are like carrier
    bags;
the only virgin to be had. (Strip-club agents cramped
in cabinet de voyeur massage their trembling
    buttocks;
fungus of stubble erupts on jowl and chin before
your very eyes; they dribble down the apricot limbs
of the painted undressed ladies on their ties.)

c) <u>Lights</u>, <u>action</u>

The unicorn raises his muzzle to taste the mad wine
running down the fleet legs of the wind.

See how she glows! Luminescent, her belly gleams
with a cold, lunar brilliance; the curious plantations
of pubic hair crackle electrically, spark
a magnesium flash.

She sings,
tunelessly: I love the game, I love the chase,
              I know and welcome each advance,
              Each sleight of foot and change of
                   place,
              Each figure in the dance.

              And then the game turns into war,
              You take out your long knife –
              Concealing what you meant it for,
              Which is, to take my life.

              I have sharp teeth inside my mouth,
              inside my dark red lips,
              And lacquer slickly hides the claws
              In my red fingertips.

So I conceal my armoury.
Yours is all on view.
You think you are possessing me –
But I've got my teeth in you.

See, he draws nearer, inexorably
drawn by the fragrance of her moist
garden plot (god wot); his little hooves
click like false teeth; he ravens
to gorge on her rich fruit-cake dark.

They sharpen knives; whisper to her
'You can put your knickers back on in a minute,
dear.'

Through the Looking Glass

Waking, Alice shook her kitten, demanding:
'Which dreamed it?' and it peed with fright;
And the nursery grew rank with metaphysics.

On the Down

Talking to a tree,
the tramp wears an earth-coloured hat.
Grave-clothes small-clothes flap
around his ankles
like little brown dogs
and he smells rusty.

He will tell you,
if you let him,
how once he was a musician
and he will play for you
an imaginary fiddle.

The tree drops
leaves
around him
as if throwing
contemptuous pennies.

William the Dreamer's Vision of Nature
[with alterations made by Carter after publication]

As I lay dreaming, then came Nature,
calling me by name, ~~unlocking~~
~~the doors of perception,~~ leading me ~~forth~~ ^(out)
to learn wisdom from the wonders of the wide world.
So, dreaming, I came to a mountain called Middle-Earth
to know love of my maker through the ways of the
    wise beasts.

I saw the sun and the sea and the salt sea strand
and birds and beasts walking with their mates,
forests where wild serpents glide and marvellous birds
shake out their ~~many-coloured~~ ^(variegated) feathers.
And man, I saw, and his mate, in plenty and poverty,
in peace and war. And joy and sorrow, together, I saw –
and how men took bribes and hardened their hearts
    against mercy.

Then I saw how Reason ruled the beasts –
their eating, their drinking, their comings-together.
When the due season for mating was done, how
    chaste they were.
Evening and morning, male walked with male, each
    to his kind,

9

no sniffing after the women, when they go great with
    young.
No cow lowed for bull, nor boar grunted after sow –
horses, nor hound, neither. All honoured generation,
except man and his mate, alas.

And I saw the small birds building in the bushes –
oh, how could a man, be he never so clever, build as
    they do?
Who taught the magpie to mesh the twigs
to cradle her eggs, where to care for her babies?
Thick human fingers can't weave so well
nor what miraculous mason make a mould for her
    nest?

Yet more I marvelled how other birds
hide up their eggs on moors and marshes, secretly,
that men may not find them. And they cover quite
their precious young from hungry eyes
if just for a moment they must leave them.

And I saw more and more birds, mating,
breeding in tree-tops, bringing forth airily, high
above ground. And the watery ones, too, I saw-
native in each element, dabchicks diving
down to moist homes in brooks, in pools.

But sadly I saw how the peacocks breed, the male
   striving
cruelly to smash the eggs, so that I feared his beauty.

But who might be the master of birds?
Who taught them the way to build so high, so safe
from man, from the wild walkers?

Then I looked on the sea and up to the stars,
and down, again, down, to the little flowers bright in
   the woods,
in the green, green grass. Some sweet, some ~~sour.~~
   ^(rank).
The smallest things are not the least marvellous.

But Reason, who ruled the beasts, governing
their doings, never controlled
man and his mate. Often they wandered, lost, lonely,
without Reason to guide them.
And this most moved me, and touched my heart
   strongest.

*freely translated from passages in William Langland's Middle
English alliterative poem 'Piers Plowman'*

Two Wives and a Widow

A modern version from the Middle Scots
of William Dunbar

If one night in the year is romantic,
that night is Midsummer's Eve. Such a night, it was ...
about midnight, I went out by myself and came
to a flower garden behind a hawthorn hedge. On a
   bough,
this crazy bird was splitting its sides,
singing. And such a scent of flowers.
The grass wet with dew, the nightingales shouting.
A night for lovers. Alone as I was,
lonely, I was. Then I heard voices,
loud, laughing voices talking in the garden.
It was a party. Whose party? So I climbed into the hedge
(though the thorns hurt dreadfully) and peered
through the branches.

       I saw three women
with flowers in their long, yellow hair, loose hair
hanging over their shoulders. They smoothed their
   green dresses
with long, white fingers – such beautiful women,
such sweet and gentle faces. Three human flowers
among the roses, the lilies. Two were married, I knew
   them –

respectable, fashionable. The other a widow.
They had a table in front of them,
with bottles and glasses,
they sat talking and drinking. And the more they
    drank,
the more they talked.
They talked freely.
            Yes, freely.

'Now,' said the widow, 'we're all girls together.
Let's play the truth game, nothing
but the truth. About husbands, our husbands,
and marriage.
            Both of you
married out of the schoolroom; any regrets?
Or did you put away pleasure
with your wedding dresses, find you'd eaten it up
with the wedding cake and not a crumb left?
What about other men?
Would you choose different if you had the chance?
And how about
the "'til death do us part" bit?'

One woman, elegant, she was, refined, said:
'Marriage!' and she spat.
'They call it blessed but I say it's hell!

I'd leave him tomorrow, if I had the chance!
A change is as good as a rest, they say;
you certainly need a rest from marriage.
            Why should it
last more than a year?
Why should two people stay
tied together when all the time they pull
            in different ways?
You know the old story – how the birds
pick a new friend each year.
The birds know the score!
            Us girls
would be in clover if we could have
a nice new boyfriend any time we liked
            and send the ones
who didn't come up to scratch packing
with a kick in the backside!
Oh, how I'd dress up
and go out and about, theatres, concerts, parties,
peacocking about, showing myself off
where all the young men were. I'd shop around
for someone to keep me warm at nights
            and then go window-shopping
for next year's boy. And he could stand in
on the current one's off-nights, when he couldn't
make it. I'd go for young boys, pretty boys,

but – you understand – capable. I'd gobble them all up,
bones and all.

I'm tied to a shadow, a worm, a blind old man
so shagged out he can't do anything but talk. He's
    nothing
but a bagfull of snot.
He can't even keep his trousers clean. He's always
scratching himself, scratching everywhere, no shame –
it's disgusting.
I could burst into tears when he kisses me.
His five o'clock shadow bristles like pig-hide (but it's
the only thing about him that can stand up to
    attention –
if you get my meaning).
            He's always talking –
oh, he can jabber away all night. But when we get
    down to it,
it's a fiasco. When he gets hold of me, it's as bad
as if some nigger bastard were jumping on me.
But I can't get away from him.
            Christ!
He's got some horrible habits,
the dirty old devil.
When he starts smirking with the love-light in his eyes
(he's got big sores all round his eyes,

they weep with pus) I could vomit all over him.
He grins and fidgets away
like a poxed old cart-horse sniffing after the mares.
But when that doddering old fool fancies a bit,
then I really get on my high horse, I do.
He can never get one hand fumbling up between my
 legs
without putting the other in his pocket.
Though he's never a bit of good to me in bed, I get
what satisfaction I can from his cheque-book,
                the morning after.
Even if he's mad for it,
I won't let him near me until he promises me a
 present –
a nice silk scarf, or a pretty new dress, or maybe a ring.
Or else he's got to go and whistle for it.
But in spite of it all, he's a bad bargain; he always
botches the job.

He's jealous, too, and spiteful. He's always on the
 watch
in case I'm getting up to mischief on the sly.
He's been randy enough in his time, he knows all the
 tricks.
And he's dying to catch me out in one of them.
He knows all right

that youth calls to youth (as they say) –
and I could rub up against him for a year and a day
and never come.

Pray God you girls don't get a husband like mine!'

How they all laughed when she finished,
and had another round of drinks.
The widow wiped her mouth and said to the other
    woman,
'How about you? How do you get on? Don't
spare us the gory details!
And I'll into the witness box after you
and tell all.'

'Now you just keep quiet about my affairs,' said the
    second,
'not a word to a soul! Thank God, no eavesdroppers.
Right.
Out with all the poison, it'll do me good.
He's a drag, a slag, a nothing, my husband.
I hate him. Yes, truly hate him.
Oh, he's young, yes, and handsome, yes –
and he used to be a great one for women, always
rolling about in some tart's bed. But that was
before I knew him.

And the consequence was,
he's sucked dry!
His thing is useless, worn out,
like an old boot that's been walked to death.
Oh, we've been to all the doctors, massage, pills,
    hormones,
psychoanalysis, even – but no joy.
And would you believe it, he still tries it on!
I've even found him trying to screw some pick-up in
    my own bed.

Not that he's got a chance. But he dresses so nicely, he's
got such a way with him, a real ladies' man – you'd
    think
he'd be at it all the time. He's always bragging
how he can make a girl come ten times without
    stopping.
Words, all words.
                He's like a dog
who can't stop sniffing the bushes, cocking
his leg though he doesn't want a pee.
But, as I said, he's handsome. Tall, dark and handsome –
dreamy. To look at.
When we got married and me so young, I thought
I'd got a gem, a jewel – but he turned out
just so much shining rubbish.

          Yes I remember.
what they say about the birds choosing new mates
every year, on Valentine's day, isn't it pretty.
If I could do like them, I wouldn't wait
until February – I'd have my legs round a new man's
     waist
and who cares what the neighbours say?

It was my family pushed me into it, damn them all –
and me so innocent, eager
for my pleasure (who isn't? that's
human nature!) I can't sleep
for brooding. Sometimes I cry.
Then he takes me in his arms (and, oh God, I can't
     help but feel
his flabby prick!) and he says: "Poor little love!
Can't she sleep?" I'm scared he'll try
something – you know – unnatural if all else fails
so I say, "No, darling, don't touch,
I've got the heartburn."
          Too true.
There's a fire in my heart.
But I've got to grin and bear it although I can't stand
     him.

The girl who'd suit him is one of the flinching kind
who's scared of it, thinks it hurts
like Mummy told her. She'd never have a moment's
    worry!
Well, I wish he'd married a girl like that,
who'd fancy no more than a bit of touching up now
    and then,
and I could climb into bed with some husky brute!'

And when she finished, once more the women laughed,
drowning their sorrows among the green leaves.
'My turn for true confessions,' said the widow.
'Now you girls listen to me
and I'll tell you how to handle a man.

            I must say,
I was always a bit of a one. But I knew how to hide it!
They always thought I was the sort of girl you'd marry,
you know what I mean! A nice girl, homely.
The fools!

            You take my advice.
Keep your noses clean. Play the "little woman".
Do what you're told, don't raise your voice, keep
your thoughts to yourself and you can rule your man
with a rod of iron! You can make his life misery
and he'll love you all the more.

And keep up appearances, dress well – it doesn't cost
    anything,
your husband'll foot the bill.

I've had two husbands and they both loved me.
Though I despised them, they never knew it.

The first had one foot in the grave. Old Father Time I
    called him.
Senile decay personified. He'd hawk and spit
    everywhere,
no control. But he never knew what I was thinking.
I was always kissing him, cuddling him, rubbing
ointment into his rheumatics, combing his hair (what
    was left
of it) – and all the time
I'd be taking the piss out of him on the quiet.
I used to have a good laugh about it
behind his back. No fool
like an old fool. He thought I stroked his wrinkles
out of love.

      Well, I had my bit of love.
He knew how to keep his mouth shut, too.
And when things got too rough with the old man,
there was always my bit of comfort, on the side.

I was clever. I had my cake and ate it too.
And my husband even thought he'd fathered
      my little boy.

After him, I married into trade.
He was middle-aged, middling height – everything
  middling.
Nothing exceptional about him except his money and
  I soon got my hands on that.
I threw myself away on him, really; and never let him
  forget it.
        I pounced on every dropped 'h';
he had a good talking to every time
he said 'serviette' or belched in company. Common,
  he was.
I used to say: "What else can you expect
from a counter-jumper?"

        I'd buried my nice ways
with my first husband. I'd talk a lot about my first –
that used to get him down. I told him straight out
what a favour I'd done him by marrying him,
only taken him on
        out of the kindness of my heart.
I had a new line, you see, and he fell for it.
He was right under my thumb.

He'd do anything to please me, fetching and carrying –
but he did nothing right.
          It's a funny thing, though,
I'd been quite fond of him when we were courting.

I was the lord and master; I ran the show.
And I despised him for letting me – fancy
being under a woman's thumb like that!
How could I respect him?
But I never let go at him completely till I'd got my
    children
named as his heirs, legally, in writing,
and his own kids by his other wife heirs
to damn all.

        After that, I ran him a race!
I even made him stay at home and keep house
and I took over his business.
He was a laughing stock.
He thought he'd try and buy me off
with all sorts of presents, Paris frocks,
scent, jewellery – nothing but the best.
I never said no. "Tak' all, gie nowt" as they say up North;
I'd get geared up like a model in the clothes he paid for
and go out looking for new lovers –
        and I found them.

When I was in bed with him, I'd
pretend it was some other man thrusting away
    inside.
Otherwise
what fun could it have been? with him?
He was never much cop.

Well, he's dead and rotten now
and I can enjoy myself quietly, in my own way.
            The world thinks
I'm grieving, still. All in black, pale but interesting,
men find me ... disturbing. I'm giving piety a whirl.
I go to church. I hide behind my prayerbook
and peek over the top at all the nice young men
            and they get the message
as often as not.

If a friend of my husband's sees me, I squeeze out a tear
    or two.
How sorry they are for me! "You can see
how much she feels it." I like
to keep things looking proper.

That's the secret – keep things looking proper.
Keep our own council, be circumspect.
Circumspect.

I've got a boyfriend on the quiet
to cheer up a poor widow, yet all the county
thinks I'm a good woman, isn't it marvellous?
       But the best of all
is at parties.
       They come flocking round me,
I'm a prize, a fine catch.
They talk so well, bring me little gifts,
make speeches, flatter me, here a kiss, there –
some of them even have the nerve,
the wicked things,
to shove themselves, stiff as a board, into my hand!
or maybe I feel it pressing against my back ...
I'm a merciful woman, I'm kind; I don't like to cause
    pain.
I pinch the ones next to me, just in fun,
lean hard on the one behind, play
footsy with another
and smile at the ones too far away for anything else.
       A bit of encouragement
doesn't do any harm.
Take one, take all – why not? I'm my own mistress.
I'd be rude to say no.

So that's the story of my life and you pay heed to the
    moral!'

The women said she was such a good teacher; they
    would
do as she said, in future. Sweetly, prudently,
they'd betray their husbands, Judas-like kissing,
    caressing,
waiting for widowhood.
Meanwhile, how dry their throats were! So they drank
    up.

Day dawned after their pleasant night. A lark singing,
a soft, fresh, melting morning, the mist dissolving.
The fields breathed clover, a skyfull of birds
    chorussing
for joy. The scent of grass, the sound
of the streams running. Clear, lovely morning –
it brings back hope, even to the saddest.

Bedtime for the elegant ladies. Home, they went,
through the flowers, yawning, and I
sat down to report their talking, as you have heard it.
Dear reader, let me put it to you.
Which of these women would you choose for your
    woman
if you should marry one of them?

From

FIVE QUIET SHOUTERS

My Cat in Her First Spring

With the spring coming, my cat is beginning to bud,
sprouting nipples all along her long, white breast,
this long-legged, adolescent she.

And in the strange
country fitfully lit by the inward-turning suns of her
    yellow
eyes, such alien trees shake out moist leaf

and the seed-crusted ferns uncoil with a slow
    blindness
in the rich fruit-cake of her dark recesses where the
    wrinkled
intuitions of her summer roses stir and tremble in
    their sleep

for spring is coming, and the fat buds bulge.

Life-Affirming Poem About Small, Pregnant White Cat

She sits (slumps); and she – bulging sack of life –
      becomes a
melting snow-cat haphazardly thrown together
by careless children. Stuffed full,
brim-full
FULL
(to the teeth)
with kittens, she yowls – and you fear an incontinent
brindled kindle will burst wrongways, out of the pink
front door.

Inside the swollen sides of the small white cat
(who suddenly, unexpectedly, finds herself so heavy she
thumps about, clattering) snugly
buttoned under two pink ranks of nipples
(such an ermine and double-breasted jacket she
      wears as used by
Shirley Temple (such an *ingénue* is she, was she but now
betrayed))
buttoned up inside her – inside (conceive!)

that taut stretched womb, crammed – some more
than base Indian black hole (is it, in there, is it like
a slit capsicum, clutch of seed hugging
the central column of an inexpressible convoluted
interior? is it like that?)

regardless – (Miracle of Everyday Things) – inside her
all the little furry commas lie blindly,
                  futurity in futurity
stirring   shifting   waiting
          to be born

The Horse of Love

The colour of the round moon is yellow, yellow
as lemons (old lemon slice moon) tumbling in dark
    leaves.
Sharp, clean and pleasing yellow; and
this is the land where the lemon trees grow.
The Horse of Love jumps over the moon, shaking
out blue mythopoeic dust from mane, from tail,
from fringed anemone eyes.

Horse (of Love) bearing
this clasped, amorous couple. Their faces, sharing
a profile, merging; the small
soft hands of the wind twining and plaiting
streamers of hair.
                And any fool knows
forepart, hindquarters, formed of two lovers (Horse
    of Love)
huddled under the hide (moths in the crutch)
slapstick old horse;
not fit for daytime, only for night, for concealing
dark, this
garish old horse, ragged old horse,
patchwork of skin of the mother-in-law that bit you,

dishcloths,
facecloths,
contraceptives, gas bills, curlers, pimples, body odour,
face cream, stained vests, sanitary towels skulking
rat-like under beds full of no rose petals but crumbs
of last night's fish-paste sandwiches and the fecund
milk bottles breeding under the sink.
etc. etc. etc.
YET:
'Yes, see – we
climb high on this pantomime horse
to squeeze the moon into our tea
and spread (green cheese) the moon on our bread.'

Poem for a Wedding Photograph (1965)

> Mary made a pudding, nice and sweet,
> Johnnie took a knife and tasted it;
> Taste, love, taste, love, don't say no.
> Next Monday morning to church we will go.

Posing for the photographer,
they stand together under a green tree
as if they were standing together for the first time
Stiffly, formally black and white, known selves,
   known bodies
subdued, submerged, lost – freshly incarnated, today,
bride and groom. And (new met in new rôles)
they smile the trembling smiles
of lone wrecked survivors, for the first time meeting,
adrift in an open boat. 'Strangers, we
embark on this strange voyage together.'
Improvise a sail (her sheathing veil); make
his body their mast. Their hands clutch.
We have only each other, now.

> Go to the East, go to the West.
> Choose the one that you love best.

Under the green tree, she
gift-wrapped in drifting white tissue, his black
lapel stuck with his badge, his white carnation.
Frozen in this eternal moment,
in the photograph, forever. Scissorred [sic] out of
the fabric of time, this icon of marriage
(like Arnolfini and his wife in the cluttered room
and the little dog, signifying fidelity).

> Clean the fire-bransticks, clean the fireside,
> Roll up the curtains, let us see the bride,
> These two lovers married in joy,
> Every year a girl or a boy.
> Under a tree, in the garden.
> A picture for a silver frame.

Poem for a Wedding Photograph (1966)

Posing for the photographer,
they stand together under a green tree
in bridal and unfamiliar clothes.
Dressed up, they are strangers to one another.
They move awkwardly, smile
the shy, nervous smiles of shipwrecked voyagers,
never met on the crowded liner till now, in the open
    boat,
embarking in embarrassment on a strange voyage,
    together,
over a strange sea. Improvise
a sail from all her satin, make a mast
out of his body. Their hands clutch, suddenly.
We have only each other. Who are we?

Under the green tree, the bride,
gift-wrapped in white. Her veil drifts in the wind,
caressing his good black suit. The shutter clicks.
They are taken. Frozen in this eternal moment,
    forever.
Scissored out of the fabric of their time,
an icon of marriage (like Arnolfini and his wife

in the cluttered room, with the little dog,
to signify fidelity).

In the garden, under a tree,
the first man and wife of all and ever,
in a silver frame, for life.

Poem for Robinson Crusoe

Such a vile beach. Dandruff sand creaks underfoot,
     shifting;
the dark tide of the unmapped black sea called 'Lack-
     of-Love'
surges (with the motion of vomiting)
sicking up its detritus all over the shore;
these bones of dead vessels grown all over (obscene
     fungus)
with used contraceptives, slimy mementoes
of life affirming impulses which never quite made
                              never quite
                                   never made it;
multiple-fractured limbs of the chair the impossible
     girl
curled impregnably in; hospital beds, ocean gone,
     bleeding rust;
crêpe bandages unfurl slowly along the water
                    ectoplasm
heraldically breast-plated with dented cans, storm-
     tossed sailors,
blanched by water, loll among sewage; their eyes
have been put out by pearls; mackerels
ate their fingers, genitals, toes, noses.

Among such leering images of romantic decay, Crusoe
judged that the best thing to do was to make a shielding
parasol against the tropic sun; then,
cannily stuffing his pockets with pearls (blind to the
empty eyeholes agape like hell's mouse runs), he
turns inland. He puts his back to the black sea
and all its symbolic refuse.

He teased sweet milk from the at-first unwilling goat.
Constructed useful pots. Dried
for raisins the hitherto Dionysiac grape (for a spotted
   dog
in the wilderness is man's best friend).

And – final triumph of man over environment – he
   taught
the lacquered flocks of parrots (aerobatic
tea trays at an evening party where he was the only
   guest)
to remind him of his identity ('Robin Crusoe!')
and hoarsely to mock his self-pity ('Poor Robin
   Crusoe!')
and thus he alienated his self-pity
after the manner of Brecht.

Shortly the wilderness shook out golden flowers,
the black sea bobbed with water-lilies,
and Crusoe sang, on Sundays, metrical versions of the
    psalms.

'JAPANESE SNAPSHOTS'

Morning Glories

At the corner shop, they put an old lady
out to air every morning. She sits
on an upright chair. She wears cracked smoked
   spectacles.
She is so old she has lapsed into a dreaming
plant life; she carries the same
weight in the world as the morning glories which
grow beside her and will fade by lunchtime.
She is kept quite clean. A child
comes out occasionally to comb her hair.
The old lady never soils her spotless
apron because she never moves.
From habit, she whispers *Irrasyaimasse*,
the shopkeeper's welcome, to passers-by,
in a dry voice, like the rustle
of a paper bag.
Her teeth are rimmed with gold.

Hannabi

I think they must love fireworks so much
because fireworks are autodestructive
but do not make any mess.

We lay down in a stubbled field
to watch the firework display.
Along the paths were stalls
where they grilled corn and cuttlefish on charcoal
or sold goldfish in plastic bags, balloons
with rabbit ears and other
gew-gaws. 'Icy, icy,
icy cream!' sang a man whose box
of wares smoked with cold.
Quiet crowds came out
to watch the fireworks, softly
squeaking children with well-brushed hair;
lovers who discreetly
dispersed in the sedge along the river.
While the darkness filled with palpable
if bourgeois magic and the fireworks
hung dissolving earrings on the night.
In this preposterous language they call them
hannabi – that is, 'flower fire'.

Only Lovers

Only lovers use this hotel, therefore
our presence here defines our status.
He checks the price per hour.
It is not unreasonable.
'Come in, come in!' says the smiling landlady.
What a cosy room! A pleasant
watercolour of a cockerel hangs
beside a capacious wardrobe which silently
reminds us to hang up our clothes tidily.
On the dresser are paper towels, a comb
and a jar of lubricating fluid. Chips
of mica glitter in the walls. The maid
brings tea and very sweet small cakes.
She wears a starched apron. She
is a model of propriety. Such a respectable brothel!
How clean the towels are. And the crisp sheets
smell of soap.
Ah! Now I understand!
This is not an illicit bedroom at all.
It is a safety-net in which the death-
defying somersault of love may be performed
with absolute propriety.
That is the custom of the country.

A SPLINTER IN THE MIND:
THE POEMS OF ANGELA CARTER

Angela Carter's reputation has had something of a switchback ride. She went, as she put it with only slight exaggeration, from being 'a very promising young writer' in the 1960s to being 'completely ignored in two novels'. Though her critical status revived in the 1980s, she never enjoyed much of what she called 'the pleasantest but most evanescent kind of fame, which is that during your own lifetime'. She was known and admired, but on nothing like the scale that has caused her to be described since her death in 1992 at the age of fifty-one as 'one of the twentieth century's best writers' and has inspired Lambeth Council to name a street in Brixton after her. Carter, who lived for much of her life in and near Brixton, loved 'melancholy down on its luck South London'. It is the setting for some of her best work and she returned to it in her last novel, *Wise Children*, which conjures up the post-war suburb with its rattling trolley buses and music halls in sad decline. She might have been as surprised by the subsequent upturn in Brixton's fortunes as by that in her own and in neither case perhaps entirely pleased, for she thrived on the marginal and contrary sides of life.

Angela Carter Close SW9 is a row of nine timber-framed houses completed in 2007. Sustainable, practical, with porches, gables and fenced front gardens, they evoke the image of home that lies deep in the English imagination and with which Carter so often made play. Their architect Anne Thorne, head of an all-woman practice, describes it as 'a new road named after the famous feminist novelist'. Yet not only has Carter's fame been erratic, her feminism is of a very particular sort. In her lifetime she was not always popular with other feminists, especially when she published her study of the Marquis de Sade in 1979. *The Sadeian Woman* is an extended essay on the man and his work that attempts to 'give the old monster his due' as a writer who 'put pornography in the service of women'. The argument won some converts but Carter was attacked from left and right by feminists and non-feminists. Her suggestion that the then recently founded feminist publisher Virago should reissue

Sade's novel *Justine* was not taken up. Today it is her originality more than her typicality of any genre she might fit – feminism, magic realism, Gothic, to choose the most obvious – that makes her work live.

Amid all the ebb and flow of opinion not much has been said about Angela Carter's poetry by anyone, including Carter herself. This was perhaps for the banal reason that she stopped writing it and, her energies having moved elsewhere, she lost interest. Her career as a published poet lasted less than a decade and was concentrated in three years from 1963 to 1966. After that came a hiatus before 'Japanese Snapshots', published in *The Listener* in 1971, marked its end. The poems deserve to be republished, not only for themselves and the light they cast on her later work but also as expressions of the historical moment that produced them. In her twenties when she wrote most of them, Carter was steeped in the forms and traditions of English verse, but she was already interested in manipulating and subverting them. Her poetry shows an extraordinary imagination finding its expression. As she once wrote of Walter de la Mare, another writer whom she championed when he was as much out of favour as Sade, albeit for different reasons, these are images that 'stick like a splinter in the mind'.

'Unicorn' is perhaps the best, certainly the most

striking, of her poems and one of the first to be published. It appeared, along with 'Through the Looking Glass', in 1963 in the magazine *Vision*. There it was called 'Allegory with a Unicorn' and the text was very slightly different from the version reproduced here. *Vision* consisted of four folded sheets held together with a single staple. It was co-edited by Carter and the poet Neil Curry from 112 Redland Road, Bristol, and is described in the British Library catalogue with unsentimental terseness: 'Poetry magazine – first and only issue'. More patronised than flattered by its acid-free cardboard jacket, the Library's copy has a forlorn air, like a scruffy guest announced by a suave butler.

'Unicorn', as it became, survived the extinction of *Vision* to be reissued in 1966 as 'A Tlaloc print-out',★ a marginally more substantial Roneoed booklet. The same year saw 'Two Wives and a Widow', Carter's version of 'The Tretis of the Tua Mariit Wemen and the Wedo', by the sixteenth-century Scots poet William Dunbar, appear in the *London Magazine*. In December she had five poems, including a much revised version of 'Poem for a Wedding Photograph', in a short anthology, *Five Quiet Shouters*, edited by Barry Tebb and published by Poet & Printer in London at two shillings.

★ Tlaloc is the Aztec god of rain.

This reappeared in 1967 as part of *One Little-Press Year*, a portfolio of poetry publications, which included Christopher Logue's *Establishment Songs*. It was less of a reissue, however, than an imaginative attempt to clear some books that had failed to sell.

Carter is a poet of the sixties, the decade when, she said, 'The pleasure principle met the reality principle like an irresistible force encountering an immovable object'. The aftershocks of the collision echo through the poems. Startling clashes of idiom and imagery set up reverberations that resound through her later work too. As Barry Tebb wrote in his introduction to *Five Quiet Shouters*, 'Miss Carter's work has a directness which at times is dizzying'. In 1966 (six years after the Chatterley trial had 'opened the floodgates of corruption', as one of Carter's characters puts it) 'women writers' were almost always so described and no woman was referred to by her surname alone unless she was a servant or a criminal. Miss Carter's work was dizzying indeed.

She had gone to university late, having formed the impression from her mother that if she was not destined for Oxford or Cambridge there was no point going at all. When she embarked on an English degree at Bristol in 1962 she was twenty-two and already knew her mind on certain points. She chose to specialise in the medieval period. Clearly, she felt an affinity for the literature, but she also found in it a refuge from the prevailing Leavisite school of criticism which had developed the least attractive aspects of F. R. Leavis's thought into a somewhat prim, prescriptive ethos. The 'eat up your broccoli' approach, Carter called it. The writers of the Middle Ages and the early modern period inhabited the literary badlands beyond the well-trodden path of Leavis's Great Tradition. A figure such as the antiquary and doctor Thomas Browne (1605–82), to whom the epigraph for 'Unicorn' is attributed, was then hardly considered to be an author at all. Carter later wrote of de la Mare that, by suggesting 'elements of religious allegory' in his work, he had 'as good as put up a "No Trespassers" sign'. In pitching her tent among writers like Dunbar and Browne she was doing something similar.

Browne belonged to an age when empiricism and the New Learning were gaining ground but what came to be called science was still interfused with theology and metaphysics. His essays and letters consider the natural world from many angles and in the conventional manner of antiquarian speculation which develops ideas by putting questions and suggesting possible answers. Browne's include ruminations on why fish don't cough (he couldn't say) and, a much debated topic in his day, whether badgers are symmetrical. (Browne thought they were.) To the unicorn, however, he could bring no first-hand observations. Although he knew that absence of evidence is not evidence of absence, and that merely 'because Dioscorides hath made no mention of unicornes horne' it did not follow that 'there is therefore no such thing in nature', he could add nothing to the myth about the use of virgins as bait. Indeed, as far as I can tell, he doesn't say anything about it at all. The lines attributed to him occur in T. H. White's *The Book of Beasts* – a translation of a twelfth-century bestiary published in 1960. Perhaps Carter, who was not always scrupulously attentive to factual detail, created from her reading of Browne and White an epigraph that is itself a piebald chimera. Against this misty background, however, the figure of the unicorn was and is still sharply defined in the common imagination. From the British royal coat of arms to the tapestries of La Dame à la licorne, source of a thousand table mats and Christmas cards, the word 'unicorn' summons up a distinct image. Mythical and yet familiar, non-existent but ubiquitous the unicorn occupies just that imaginative ground that Carter was always to inhabit as a writer, the 'magical and enigmatic ... space of the invisible' as she called it, between dreams and different kinds of consciousness.

Thus at the age of twenty-three she arrived, as it were in a single bound, in the middle of the mysterious forest that was to keep her supplied with ideas for the rest of her life. Having arrived, she at once set about assembling her dramatis personae in the most literal sense: 'bend the tab, slit in slot marked "x"'. Like the cut-outs in a children's toy theatre, these are not meant to be actors or figures in the round, they are agents, manipulated by an unseen hand. That is what myth and tradition offer, a kind of flat-pack of pre-existing characters and stories to be reconfigured every so often according to the needs of a different age. Carter believed that a narrative was 'an argument stated in fictional terms' and she often presented her protagonists as intellectual positions with their allegorical and moral values stamped on their foreheads. If they have a state of mind it is not internalised; they are themselves a state of mind personified. They often have labels rather than names and they do as she tells them. She once said she had no patience with writers who claimed that their characters took over the plot, this was, in her view, bad authorial management.

Meanwhile, in the magic forest of 'Unicorn', the mechanism has been assembled and the figures come to a kind of awkward life. The unicorn blossoms out from the flat field of tapestry, his horn swelling into its full glory in the mysterious twilight. In the first version of the poem the horn is 'ithyphallic', but Carter may have felt that was labouring the point and she dropped the word. (Although she kept it by her and found a place for it in her first novel, Shadow Dance.) The virgin too is both more and less than her needlepoint original. She is rounder, larger, 'huge', in fact, like many later Carter women, but not a beauty, or even particularly attractive. 'Breasts like carrier bags' is not the happiest of images. Carrier bags, after all, are often square, and even if round it isn't clear whether these are full or empty. In either case, however, the effect is successfully unappealing and anti-erotic. The iconography slithers down from illuminated manuscript to strip cartoon as the virgin's despair emerges in a thought balloon 'on a chain of bubbles'.

In the margins of the clearing in the wood the strip-club agents, imagining themselves concealed, are visible to the narrative eye. All that seems to the twentieth century to be latent in the unicorn myth of sex and violence is about to be made as luridly explicit as a flashing neon sign outside a porn shop: 'Lights, action'. The prescribed events unfold, the virgin's tuneless song, 'I've got my teeth in you', with its jog-trot metrics parodies popular love lyrics, which are so often macabre if taken literally: 'I've got you under my skin', 'You took the part that once was my heart', 'Where did you get those eyes?' The virgin as she starts to move is a clattering synecdoche, a machine of female accoutrements, lacquered nails and teeth set in a dark red mouth that is meant for that other mythic trope the *vagina dentata*. And so one myth attracts another, the unicorn is lured, his clacking hooves like false teeth drawn towards her real teeth, and he is caught. The virgin, still (just) a virgin, is redundant and abandoned to bathos: 'You can put your knickers back on in a minute, dear.'

Writing of her time in Japan in the 1970s Carter said that her physical difference from the Japanese made her stand out like 'a kind of phoenix, a fabulous beast', so that she often 'felt like a female impersonator'. The idea that all women are to some extent drag artists, assemblages of parts, reflections of received images that turn them into emblematic figures, was already there in her work. In an early story 'The Man Who Loved a Double Bass', a musician adores his instrument 'with a deep and steadfast passion'. It has the shape of 'a full-breasted, full-hipped woman, recalling certain primitive effigies of the Mother Goddess so gloriously essentially feminine was she, stripped of irrelevancies of head and limbs'. Like a sex doll, the bass is unable to walk away or answer back. The fetishisation of female body parts in images from pornography to icons of the Virgin, reaches a point where, as Carter wrote in *The Sadeian Woman*, breasts and buttocks 'become the signs of a denaturised being ... As surprising and unusual physical appurtenances ... as fins or wings', and in *Nights at the Circus* she went so far as to give the aerialist Fevvers actual wings, which may or may not be false.

Like Swift and Carroll, two of her most frequently invoked literary influences, she deploys non- or semi-human creatures to great effect. Mechanical simulacra move the action on in much of her fiction. Even unambiguously human characters like Honeybuzzard in *Shadow Dance* have a penchant for false noses and plastic teeth. Melanie in *The Magic Toyshop* is terrified as a child by a jack-in-the-box with her own face on it. This splitting, mirroring, the anatomising of identity, are all there already in 'Unicorn'. But where is Carter, the controlling narrator? In 'Flesh and the Mirror', another of the 'profane pieces' based on her years in Japan which are part story, part memoir, she wrote that she had felt 'as if there were glass between me and the world'.

I could see myself perfectly well on the other side of the glass. There I was, walking up and down, eating meals, having conversations, in love, indifferent, and so on. But all the time I was pulling the strings of my own puppet ... and I eyed the most marvellous adventures with the bored eye of the agent with the cigar watching another audition. I tapped out the ash and asked of events: 'What else can you do?'

Carter is the virgin and the strip-club voyeur and so are we.

The coupling of complicit opposites, voyeurs and exhibitionists, sadists and masochists, men and women locked in the tango of sexual politics are enduring themes. Who controls whom, who is writing the drama and who is the actor? These questions are constantly revolved. In the other poem in *Vision* it takes the form of the final chapter of *Through the Looking Glass*, 'Which Dreamed It?'. In Carroll's version Alice asks her kitten whether the dream has been hers or the Red King's and is answered with an enigmatic purr. The glass becomes solid again, the two worlds divide and the story ends. Carter's Alice is more violent. She shakes the stupid kitten and when it 'peed with fright' the dream world and the material world spilled messily back into one another, 'the nursery grew rank with metaphysics'. There is no tidy ending.

Carroll also casts a shadow in 'Unicorn', for fruit-cake is quite undreamt of in Thomas Browne's philosophy of unicorn habits. It must be a preference acquired in the pages of *Through the Looking Glass*. There the nursery-rhyme roles of the Lion and the Unicorn are, naturally, reversed. The Lion instead of beating the Unicorn retires hurt. Carroll's Unicorn is the winner, a slouching, caddish Flashman type who saunters into view, hands in his pockets. At the sight of Alice he 'turned round instantly, and stood for some time looking at her with an air of the deepest disgust'. In this confrontation of fabulous beast and virgin, there is no suggestion of sex or attraction, but a symmetrical state of incredulity. The Unicorn always thought that children were merely mythical and Alice thought the same about unicorns. 'Well, now that we **have** seen each other,' said the Unicorn, 'if you'll believe in me, I'll believe in you. Is that a bargain?' It is. It is the bargain every storyteller makes with every reader or listener, the compact of mutual confidence on which the tale depends and which Carter strikes so disturbingly with her readers.

Her next three poems appeared in the *Aylesford Review* in 1965. It was a significant choice of publication. The *Review*, edited by the Carmelite monk Father Brocard Sewell, was one of many remarkable productions to emanate from Aylesford Priory in Kent in the decades after the Second World War. A Carmelite house, founded in 1242 and refounded in 1949, more than four centuries after it had been dissolved at the Reformation, Aylesford was redolent of a peculiarly English compound of idealism, radical politics and handcraft, with a touch of mysticism. The legacies of William Morris and Eric Gill were developed in the Priory's buildings by Adrian Gilbert Scott, in stained glass, furniture and ceramics by the monks and others, including the Polish artist and refugee Adam Kossowski, who made the astonishing black and white ceramic reliquary for the skull of St Simon Stock. In 1965 Father Sewell arrived at Aylesford by what one fellow Carmelite described laconically as 'a series of diversions', whereupon he started a library, a press and the *Review*. A man of strong and often conflicting convictions, he created a magazine that fought for civil liberties while it mapped the post-war literary world. In its pages the end of Edwardian careers, like that of John Cooper Powys, overlapped with the post-war avant-garde in the work of Michael Hastings, Colin Wilson, Muriel Spark and Carter herself.

The poems she published here have a softer edge than those that come before and after, an elegiac note that perhaps reflects the idiosyncratic spirituality of the Aylesford enterprise. 'On the Down' sets going a character, half-derelict half-shaman, whose halting career she took up three years later in a novel. *Several Perceptions*, begins with the tramp, his 'grave-clothes' flapping, 'gilded with visionary sunset light' as if 'just dropped from heaven'. 'Poem for a Wedding Photograph', an early experiment in combining her own narrative with traditional rhymes and stories, is interesting for that reason, but in its revised version of 1966 is more coherently successful. The third of the *Aylesford Review* poems, 'William the Dreamer's Vision of Nature' is, like 'Unicorn', a revisiting of the medieval world, this time the Middle Earth of Piers Plowman. It is, as she says, 'freely translated' from Book or *Passus* XI of William Langland's poem. A vision both lyrical and disturbing, in which the beauty of the world and the ingenuity of its creatures is flecked with corruption, like shards of glass in spun sugar. The venality and lust of man contrast with the rationality of the animals, but even here, in the peacock, is a glimpse of violence and destruction. The male bird's supposed habit of breaking its eggs in order to go on enjoying his mate for longer is not spelled out in Langland. Carter brings it up from the footnotes to sound an extra undertone of unease.

A year later she turned her attention to another medieval view of mating rituals, the conventions of courtly love. Published in England's oldest literary periodical *The London Magazine*, 'Two Wives and a Widow' offers a more deeply sceptical view of sex and human nature, for which she found a ready-made accomplice in William Dunbar. Her 'modern version from the Middle Scots' of his *Tretis of the Tua Mariit Wemen and the Wedo* is considerably shorter than the original, however, and in some ways more decorous. Dunbar's poem was written some time between 1500 and 1513. A satire on the conventions of marriage and chivalric love, it is set in a garden at midnight on Midsummer's Eve. Here the anonymous narrator comes upon a party of ladies, whose conversation he overhears and duly relays to the reader. So far so entirely in keeping with the tropes of contemporary literature. The three women he eavesdrops on are kin to the Lady of the Unicorn. Like figures in a book of hours, they sit in a green arbour and are as lovely as the flowers in their glittering golden hair. Before them is a table with glasses and fine wine. Female trios are common in myth, whether graces or witches, but these three turn out to be boozy, brassy blondes. As the bottle goes round and the conversation turns to marriage and thence to sex, the conventions are kicked over, the language gets graphic, the real women come out from behind the masks of decorum and, as befits midsummer, the world is turned upside down.

Dunbar was a salaried poet or 'mackar' at the court of James IV and his readers were sophisticated enough to recognise the satirical tradition in which he was working. A good deal of the comedy is in the play with registers of speech and verse. The middle of the poem is a vernacular lyric and it is rammed up at both ends against the courtly high style of the introduction and conclusion. The mixing of voices and genres creates a linguistic slapstick. Sudden swerves of tone make the reader do a double take or crash into a pratfall from the sublime to the ridiculous. Bathos always delighted Carter. She was deploying it already in 'Unicorn'. She probably knew Dunbar's poem when she wrote it and although she only translated his work verbatim once, she translated his methods into contemporary terms over and over again. Her wide ranging literary allusions to Swift, Defoe and Shakespeare are larded with music hall songs, filmic shifts of perspective and cockney.

She believed that 'our lives are all about our childhoods' and she spent a lot of hers in the cinema, specifically at the Tooting Granada, where her father took her to see whatever was showing, thereby introducing her to some formatively unsuitable material. Film, the only art form created in the twentieth century, was an inexhaustible source of imagery. She ranged through genres from Art House to Wild West. The poems she published in *Vision* appeared over the pseudonym Rankin Crowe, a name I found puzzling until Carter's biographer Edmund Gordon explained that Crow (without the 'e') was an early twentieth-century cowboy, author of a memoir, *Rankin Crow and the Oregon County.* 'Angela,' he adds, 'was into cowboys – she saw *A Fistful of Dollars* more than once.' In Tooting, however, it was not just the films but the cinema itself that caught her imagination. Like its sister Granada at Woolwich, its fabulous Gothic interior was created by the Russian theatre and opera designer Theodore Komisarjevsky (1882–1954).

Komisarjevsky, briefly artistic director of the Bolshoi, became an exile from the Soviet regime and his later career ricocheted between Paris, London and Stratford-on-Avon, taking in several marriages, including one to Peggy Ashcroft, on the way. He was brought in by the Granada cinema chain to help them establish a house style that would contrast with the sleek art deco faience tiles and monochrome exteriors of the Odeons. The brief was fulfilled on a scale beyond anything they could have anticipated. Komisarjevsky's auditoria are expressionist confections, part cathedral, part Fabergé egg, whose tinselly riches hint in the half-light at further depths. The mixture of fakery, exoticism and glamour, subdued light glinting on speckled mirrors and chipped gilt, at once fabulous and suburban, was the arena in which Carter first rehearsed her imaginary dramas.

The collision of ideal love and petty sexual politics in Dunbar's poem is reconfigured in Carter's. If 'Two Wives and a Widow' were a film it would be a mash-up of *Brief Encounter* and *Carry on Camping*. She is so in tune with Dunbar that she takes few liberties with him as a source. Her version is if anything too respectful to succeed as an independent poem. It is a pity, for example, that she held back from reworking the first wife's inventively insulting description of her elderly husband. Where Carter has:

> 'a shadow, a worm, a blind old man
> so shagged out he can't do anything but talk. He's
>   nothing
> but a bagfull of snot.'

Dunbar says the same, though his alliterative style gives it more punch, but then goes on to let the first wife elaborate:

> 'ane wallidrag, ane worme, an auld wobat carle,
> A waistit wolroun, na worth bot wourdis to clatter;

Ane bumbart, ane dron bee, ane bag full of flewme,
Ane skabbits karth, ane scorpioun, ane scatarde
behind'

'Bumbart' is particularly good. When we get to the husband's performance in bed it is Carter again who is coy.

Dunbar's

'As birs of ane brymbair, his berd is als stif,
Bot soft and soupill as the silk is his sary lume'

has nothing of euphemism. Literally it might be 'His beard is stiff as a wild boar but his apology for a dick is soft and floppy as silk'. In Carter it becomes a nudge-and-wink joke:

'His five o'clock shadow bristles like pig-hide (but
it's
the only thing about him that can stand up to atten-
tion –
if you get my meaning).'

Perhaps she felt that readers of the London Magazine in 1966 were more easily offended than the court of James IV and perhaps she was right.

The subtlest aspect of her poem is not the translation from Middle Scots to modern English but the translation from a male to a female poet. Dunbar is a man portraying a man watching women. Carter is a woman impersonating a man portraying another man, watching women. As in 'Unicorn', the layers multiply. She is narrator and voyeur and, being on all sides, is on none – certainly not that of the women. The poem's consideration of marriage as ideal and as reality does not exactly flatter the female character. If the husbands are preposterous the wives are unscrupulous. They use the weapons of the weak: deceit and manipulation. They exploit their sexuality for all it is worth and, having got their own way, despise the men they've outwitted. The portrayal of female whimsicality, for preferring the chase to the capture, is summed up with devastating understatement: 'It's a funny thing, though, /I'd been quite fond of him when we were courting.' Carter's women, here and in her other work, are wronged, but they are also often wrong, collaborators as much as victims. It is not men only, but the whole interwoven construct of social relations that is under scrutiny.

The poems in *Five Quiet Shouters*, published at the end of 1966, mark a climax, a new assurance and at the same time the beginning of something else, for by then Carter's first novel had appeared. In the poems the same devices recur and are developed: nursery rhymes and another author's creature, this time Robinson Crusoe, virgins, a bride, Adam and Eve, kittens and a pantomime horse – the cast and the settings are becoming familiar and will soon move on to be leitmotivs in her prose. In verse Carter has them now well enough in hand to manoeuvre them with confidence and economy. The cat, queasily full of kittens, is a matryoshka doll stuffed with condensed images: the violated virgin, the child star Shirley Temple, the sexy yet repulsive fruit-cake of generative organs and kittens, 'futurity in futurity'. She is also, with her nipples like the buttons of 'an ermine and double-breasted jacket', Puss in Boots in waiting. These are not, as the irony implicit in the title of the second cat poem implies, 'life-affirming' images except in so far as they affirm the unstoppable and uncontrollable force of biological life. They are queasy and uneasy. Only in 'Poem for a Wedding Photograph', revised and purged of its folk rhyme interpolations, is there something like tenderness for the couple who are archetypes 'the first man and wife of all and ever', but also shy and in their vulnerability almost human by Carter's standards.

For the most part in these poems the 'lemon slice

moon' and the 'inward-turning suns' of the cat's eyes light a dystopian landscape littered with filth. On the one hand there is the squalid banality of everyday life, 'face cream, stained vests, sanitary towels skulking/ rat-like under beds' and on the other its homely comforts, steamed puddings and metrical psalms. In between come flashes of the fantastic, parrots as aerobatic tea trays bring another echo of Carroll ('like a tea tray in the sky'). Had sanitary towels appeared in poetry before? Perhaps not and perhaps they were what made Barry Tebb dizzy. The wreckage on the shore of Crusoe's reimagined island is the debris of the 1960s, the great collision of precepts and principles.

In turning to prose Carter lost nothing of her gift for the telling image. One of her translators later described her writing as 'embroidery' so fine were the details. Sometimes they are, the 'sequin regard' of a cat, Fevvers's discarded corset 'like the pink husk of a giant prawn', a character with eyes that are 'no colour like a rainy day'. At other times the imagery is bulbous, more like the gobstopper marbles in the sides of a High Victorian font. In *Several Perceptions* (published in 1968), Mrs Boulder, the decaying prostitute and barmaid, despondent after some ill-advised sex in front of the electric fire, 'lay in a pool of lace, huge, white and wounded as a shot swan'. Dunbar would have enjoyed the alliteration. But Carter's desire for narrative was better served by prose fiction and in 1966 she published *Shadow Dance*, and became a 'promising young writer'.

It was a good year for it. The Beatles had put young writers in the charts:

> It's the dirty story of a dirty man
> And his clinging wife doesn't understand ...
> It's a steady job but he wants to be a paperback writer

Writing novels as a way of avoiding deadly steady jobs, the gritty account of the life of face cream and stained vests that could buy its author out of it, was now an established phenomenon. As Carter wrote in *Shadow Dance*, 'young girls with high pitched voices in plays about unhappy marriages among the lower middle classes' were now regularly to be heard 'on the Home Service on Wednesday afternoons'.

ANGRY YOUNG MEN AND DISGUSTING GIRLS:
WRITING IN THE 1960S

Classing Carter as a 'sixties writer' is as limiting as classing her as a feminist or a magic realist but, as she says in *The Sadeian Woman*, 'One may not remove oneself from history'. The historical circumstances of her early work fed into what she wrote and are reflected back in the books with which she made her name. The 1960s were not, indeed, like the movies. They were more complicated. The generation then in their twenties were the children of wartime and rationing. They experienced the clash of the pleasure principle and the reality principle within themselves, and in Carter this found expression in a combination of the subversive and the strait-laced that runs through her writing. Her early childhood, during the war, was spent mostly in

Yorkshire with her grandmother and she remembered its 'mild discomfort' with approval: 'the fact that you were always a little bit healthily cold, and yet you had brown bread' suited a temperament of which high thinking and plain living were to be enduring characteristics. Eight years older than the National Health Service, she grew up with the welfare state: 'all that free milk and orange juice and cod liver oil', a no-nonsense view of life that manifested as a certain briskness of tone applied to the most surprising subjects. Not many people would complain of the Marquis de Sade that he 'dithers'. Along with such pragmatism Carter's writing deploys a kaleidoscope of fantastical imagery, often combined with extreme violence, much of it sexual. Looking back from the 1980s, she was 'quite appalled' by some of what she had written. Where it came from seemed to puzzle her.

In terms of external influence it is easy enough to see: like her poetry, it had roots in film, in Swift and Lewis Carroll and in the Middle Ages, but it had other non-Anglophone sources. Psychoanalysis, the theatre of the absurd, existentialism, surrealism, the poetry of Apollinaire all interested her. They offered linguistic and narrative possibilities for exploring those divided, altered and half-conscious states of mind where she felt most at home as a writer, especially when she was

writing about extremes of experience. They also ena-
bled her to escape the Leavisite ideal, as she saw it, of
'real' novels in which people, 'drank tea and commit-
ted adultery'. If there was an opposite of the Great Tra-
dition view of culture it was to be found in post-war
Paris, where all those currents of Continental art and
thought flowed together. While Carter was writing her
first fiction she was inhabiting the 'provincial bohe-
mia of Bristol and Bath' and trying, Paul Barker recalls,
in his entry on Carter in the *Oxford Dictionary of National
Biography* 'to live as much like a French left bank habit-
uée as she could ... styling herself like Juliette Greco
and admiring the films of Godard'.

The West Country in the mid-1960s was bathed in
the backwash of the Anglo-American-French bohemia
that emerged on the Parisian Left Bank a decade earlier
and whose literary and other productions helped
shaped Carter's imaginative repertoire. Like all bohe-
mias, it was in constant flux, loyal to no consistent ide-
ology and delighted to twist the tails of *bien pensants* of
left or right. It is at this point that Carter's path again
crosses that of Christopher Logue. Christopher was in
Paris on and off from 1951 to 1956, part of a group of
aspiring writers and industrious translators, mostly
English or American. They belonged to the generation
before Carter's that had had its youth interrupted by

war and was not willing, yet, to settle into middle age. In Paris they could live cheaply and American ex-servicemen who were on the GI Bill, the law that provided benefits for returning veterans including a year's unemployment compensation, were relatively rich. The literary output of the Paris expatriates and their circle ranged from Beckett's *Watt* to the Traveller's Companion series of cheap pornography.

Much of what they wrote was published and some of it commissioned by Maurice Girodias (1919–90), the self-described 'Anglo-French pornographer'. A lot has been written about Girodias and the best of it is listed at the end of this volume. In summary, between 1953 and 1964, under various imprints including Olympia, Collection Merlin and the Ophelia Press, he published *Watt* and the English versions of Beckett's later novels *Molloy*, *Malone Dies* and *The Unnamable*, Nabokov's *Lolita*, J. P. Donleavy's *The Ginger Man*, *The Black Diaries of Roger Casement*, *The Story of O* (in English translation) and the first complete English translations of Sade's *Justine* and *The 120 Days of Sodom* – 'Anything,' Girodias said, 'that shocks because it comes before its time, anything that is liable to be banned by the censors because they cannot accept its honesty.' Christopher's first poems were published by Girodias. His closest friends in Paris were the Scot Alex Trocchi, translator of Apollinaire and co-editor of *Merlin* (the magazine that published Beckett), and the American Austryn Wainhouse, translator of Sade. Beckett had started the job but was making slow progress. Austryn, scrupulous and dogged, saw it through and produced the complete versions that Carter later used in her attempt to turn Sade into a very particular kind of feminist.

Girodias's publications offered a virtual reading list for the avant-garde of 1960s Britain. The exotic combination of intellectualism, sex, symbolism and scatological realism is like nothing much in Anglo-Saxon literature, but it is like a great deal in Angela Carter. The combination of glamour and decadence she first glimpsed in the Tooting Granada was realised on a grand scale, if briefly, by Girodias in La Grande Séverine, his 'futuristic, multi-levelled nightclub' in Paris. This 'toy', as he called it, was opened in 1958 with the profits from *Lolita* and closed five years later by the Vice Squad when he attempted to put on a theatrical adaptation of Sade's *Philosophy in the Boudoir*.

The economics of Girodias's operations were inevitably precarious. Slim volumes of poetry did not pay and poets wanting their work published had to fund it by writing pornography for the steady sellers in the Traveller's Companion series. Christopher's contribution to Girodias's output in both categories was not large. His first book of poems, *Wand and Quadrant*, appeared in 1953 and was a modest success. Ezra Pound wrote to say it was 'not bad'. His efforts at pornography, however, were more fraught. Girodias, who provided the authors of his dirty books with pseudonyms, named Christopher 'Count Palmiro Vicarion' and under that name he wrote a novel, *Lust*, of which he was later deeply ashamed, on literary rather than moral grounds. It is not a good book. It now has to be read on the same desk of 'Restricted Material' in the British Library as Carter's earliest poems and it has a similarly embarrassed air. Whatever power it had to shock is as faded as its once-pink cover.

Christopher's original idea for a dirty book, however, was much better (and very Carteresque). It was to be called *The Abominable Circus*. 'It was to feature,' he recalled, 'a troupe of sexual gold-medallists performing singly, in pairs, trios, quartets, or even larger combinations, on horse and/or elephant back, up on the high wire; swinging from the trapeze or while being fired from cannons. Their pan-European adventures were to be set in the seventeenth century' and, though hugely popular with the public, they were to be relentlessly pursued by the Papal Secret Police. Girodias was unimpressed. 'This,' he said, 'will never do. You are not writing pornography to amuse yourself.' So

Christopher went on with the more conventional sort of dirty book and, since he was paid by the chapter and since Girodias was insistent on ever more sex and ever less surreal comedy, the narrative of *Lust*, such as it is, veers wildly. At the end Girodias inserted an exquisitely dry publisher's note:

> The reader may have noted a disconcerting change of tone in the course of Count Vicarion's narrative. This is unfortunately explained by the cruel mental struggle sustained by the great Byzantine writer at the time of the composing of the present work of fiction. It nevertheless remains as a touching demonstration of his artistic integrity and of his knoweldge [*sic*] of the human heart.

This miniature is much more convincing than the novel and in it the Count, just for a moment, becomes a character, one of those tragic or sinister Middle European figures set adrift by the traumas of the twentieth century, who haunt the reimagined fairy tales in *The Bloody Chamber*.

It could not be said that the bohemian Left Bank of the mid-fifties was feminist, but it did involve women. Iris Owens wrote pornographic novels under the nom de plume Harriet Daimler. *Merlin* was supported financially by Jane Lougee. *The Story of O*, an extrapolation from Sade which also interested Carter and which was simultaneously banned and awarded the important literary Prix des Deux Magots, was by the French writer Anne Desclos. By contrast the avant-garde in England, when Carter was growing up, presented a much more blokish and provincial appearance in the shape of the Angry Young Men. They were different from the Leavisites, more beer than broccoli, but they had little to offer a writer of Carter's cast of mind.

In so far as they had any existence as an entity, the Angry Young Men were a reality for at most two years. The term seems to have been coined in 1956 by an exasperated press officer at the Royal Court theatre struggling to describe John Osborne, whose *Look Back in Anger* was then in rehearsal. Osborne, he said, was an 'angry young man'. The phrase was taken up by the *Evening Standard*, repeated by Osborne himself and soon became the subject of opinion pieces with titles like: 'Today's Angry Young Men'. Kingsley Amis, John Wain, John Braine and Colin Wilson made up, with Osborne, the core of a grouping that was never a group. Many of the supposed members disliked the others, often attacked one another's work and in their personal pronouncements ran the gamut of bad temper from righteous anger to peevishness.

In 1958, the year La Grande Séverine opened in Paris, the Angries put in a final appearance. It was at the Royal Court theatre during a performance of Stuart Holroyd's play *The Tenth Chance*, a 'spiritual drama' based on the true story of a Roman Catholic lorry driver from Oslo. Christopher (who was back from Paris and, though he disliked being associated with the Angry Young Men, knew them all) was there and found the play boring and pretentious. Towards the end he shouted 'Rubbish!', which got a laugh. He had a very distinctive voice and Anne Hastings, first wife of the playwright Michael Hastings, replied from the stalls: 'Christopher Logue, get out of this theatre.' Which got a bigger laugh.

As the cast struggled to ensure that the show should go on Christopher and his friend Elaine Dundy, wife of the critic Ken Tynan, adjourned to the pub next door, where they were joined by the rest of the audience after the curtain came down for an exchange of obscure insults. Christopher remembered Anne Hastings launching herself at him and saying that she would crush him with her Daimler. Tynan said to Colin Wilson, 'Get out of my life', and Dundy removed a shoe and said, 'Don't worry about the women, Christopher I'll deal with them'. In fact, it was barely a brawl. Christopher thought nobody was hit, but it got the idea of the Angries into the newspapers again, and for pretty much the last time as a going concern. After that they survived chiefly as a critical and soon an historical term.

As individuals some produced enduring work, but as a phenomenon the most important thing about them was, as Michael Ratcliffe suggests in his essay in the *Oxford Dictionary of National Biography*, that they happened at all. In weary, often dreary, claustrophobic and repressed post-war Britain, the voice of protest had been raised and the possibility of change and renewal came to seem more real. It remained, however, a very male vision. Ratcliffe's character sketch of the typical Angry-Young-Man hero is the reverse of the Paris bohemian: a beer drinker from a provincial town with 'a very English distaste for "abroad"', a man who loves women, but finds them 'like the reforms of the new welfare state, emasculating'. They were soon to find them much more so. As the 1960s went on the idea of an avant-garde gave way to a multiplicity of views and visions. The neo-Romantic Radical utopianism of the *Aylesford Review* was one manifestation, CND another and the turn of the decade also saw the emergence of a remarkable number of talented young women writers who made some of the Angry Young Men simply furious.

In the year of the Sloane Square shouting match the shoe-wielding Dundy published a novel, *The Dud Avocado*, that brought together the Left Bank and the English avant-garde. It is a very funny book, based on the year that Dundy, a New Yorker, had spent living in Paris, where she hung out with the ex-pats, casting a quizzical eye over a scene she found less romantic and stimulating than it was cracked up to be. 'I reflected wearily,' her heroine Sally Jay remarks, 'that it was not easy to be a Woman in these stirring times.' At frugal dinners, mostly with fellow Americans, the cuisine was based to a depressing extent on aubergines, while the conversation never got going until 'the last dish had been cleared away and we women were busy at the sink washing up ... After that we were allowed to listen to the menfolk for a while and after that it was bed-time'. *The Dud Avocado* was a best seller and Dundy hoped her husband would be pleased. In fact, however stifled she had felt by the men in Paris, she fared worse in London. Tynan was incensed by his wife's growing reputation as a writer. Their marriage broke down and finally ended in 1964.

By then a number of significant novels by new women writers had been published, though their authors were not seen by anyone, including themselves, as a group or a movement. They brought fresh and to some people frightening areas of experience into the mainstream of paperback fiction. Lynne Reid Banks's *The L-Shaped Room*, Muriel Spark's *The Ballad of Peckham Rye* and Edna O'Brien's *The Country Girls* were all published in 1960. In 1961 came *The Prime of Miss Jean Brodie*, in 1962 Doris Lessing's *The Golden Notebook* and in 1963 Sylvia Plath's *The Bell Jar*, Spark's *The Girls of Slender Means* and Nell Dunn's short-story collection *Up the Junction*. By 1966, when Carter's *Shadow Dance* came out, it was quite possible for a paperback writer to be a woman. But it had come at a cost. While the men had had all the fun of épating the bourgeoisie in ways that cost them little and made their reputations, the women had a real fight. Maybe nobody got hit in the pub in Sloane Square but by the time Dundy left Tynan she had sustained a broken nose and two black eyes.

Carter, who was not always the most perceptive critic of her contemporaries, had less time than she might have done for the 'heart-struck, tearful heroines' of Edna O'Brien, so different from Carter's own protagonists. But O'Brien had had to be brave. Like Dundy, she found her husband was repelled by her success. 'You can write and I will never forgive you,' he told her when *The Country Girls* was published, thus ringing 'the death-knell of the already ailing marriage'. Her mother at home in Ireland told her of the 'hurt and disgust' the book had caused among their friends and neighbours. The Archbishop of Dublin, John Charles McQuaid, was in horrified correspondence with Charles Haughey, then Irish Minister of Justice, on the subject of the 'filth' that was *The Country Girls*. Like the Archbishop of Westminster, the two men were baffled that it had not been universally condemned. The publisher's advertisement for Nell Dunn's *Poor Cow*, which appeared in the back of the Pan paperback edition of Carter's first novel, took full account of the mixture of titillation and indignation that these young women writers aroused. 'This sizzling novel,' they promised, was about 'a girl who snatches sex and excitement anywhere she can.' Below that is a quote from John Braine: 'I was disgusted, I was nauseated, I was saddened but I was not bored.' It was a back-handed compliment: Nell had further annoyed an habitually Angry Young Man, but without committing the ultimate feminine sin of boring him.

The women writers, artists and thinkers of the 1960s were threatening, to both men and women, in a way that the Angries never really were. Men had always done the shouting and the fighting. Poets had long been mad and bad. With women it was different. Looking back on that time, Nell recalls that 'the lid was still down very tight' on women and what they could do. She felt isolated as an aspiring writer stuck at home in Putney with a small baby. Her husband, the screen-writer Jeremy Sandford, best remembered for *Cathy Come Home*, told her she was not to come with him to a party because since giving birth she had become 'a vegetable'. In an attempt to find out how other women who had ambitions to write or paint or generally do more than housework managed their lives, Nell conducted a remarkable series of interviews. *Talking to Women*, published in 1965, records verbatim conversations with nine women whose interests ranged, according to the publishers' blurb, over topics including 'sex, babies, morals, careers, freedom – and men', an order of priorities that, like the advertisement for *Poor Cow*, says more about the publishers than the book. *Talking to Women* is a collaged group portrait composed at the halfway point of a much mytholo-gised decade.

Many of the transcripts convey the slightly clipped RP tones of the period. Nell's interlocutors are hesitant and say 'one' a lot but most of the topics covered would have been recognisable to William Dunbar. 'Do you think marriage is a completely hypocritical state of affairs?' Nell asks the novelist Ann Quin. 'Well it seems to be all around us, doesn't it,' is the somewhat grim reply. Exploitation of the male sex drive as a diversionary tactic is there too. While Quin complains about being assessed physically more often than intellectually Nell suggests this has its advantages, 'because it's such an easy role to play the physical role. In a way you get over them by playing that role'. On the whole, though, these women are nicer, kinder and feel very much more guilty than the Two Wives and the Widow. Their fifteenth-century predecessors had to accept the status quo and had no scruples about undermining it from within. These women were both freer and less certain. 'I don't know how I am meant to behave in any given situation,' Nell remarks to the pop artist Pauline Boty, who struggles in reply to describe her own ambivalence about disregarding conventions with a disarming directness that suggests what the sixties were often really like:

There's no kind of – there isn't a real tradition about it, you see. It isn't sort of things that have grown up. For instance one moment you might be going to somewhere where there's a load of smart people and the next moment you're with a lot of artists – you know, it's just sort of like that.

On the question of motherhood and work Edna

O'Brien, older and more battle-hardened than Nell and Boty, a divorcee now with four novels and two sons, was clearer, but not much more optimistic:

> Half the time I felt I ought to be buying bones and scraping the marrow out ... and really being a mother and the other half I want not to know that they're alive ... at our peril, or at a woman's peril she takes this on and that's why women's books and writing, modern women read as screams ... I think women who write should not have children.

Just how threatening this all seemed, to other women as well as to men, in 1965 and how far outside the social mainstream O'Brien and others had put themselves is clear in a review of *Talking to Women* by Mary Conroy. These women 'with that capital W' annoyed her. 'Mainly writers, artists and actresses, they come from a milieu they describe as "the art world",' she noted. She was impatient with the fact that they aspired to 'having children *and* feeling free from them'. The result of this sort of behaviour, Conroy concluded, could only be 'looseness and paucity'. Even sympathetic men were baffled. Nell recalls Karl Miller, her editor at the *New Statesman*, asking with genuine curiosity: 'Isn't it enough for you to look after your child?' It was no wonder that so much of the writing and the painting came out as a scream and Conroy was not entirely wrong to suggest that Women with a capital W would come to no good.

For Dundy and O'Brien, their determination to write had already led to divorce. Nell and Jeremy Sandford also parted and eventually divorced. When in 1969 Carter won the Somerset Maugham Prize, awarded to young writers to fund foreign travel, she used it to go to Japan, leaving her husband in the process, something she thought Maugham would have approved of. Not everyone got away. Two of the nine women Nell talked to, Ann Quin and Frances Chadwicke, took their own lives aged thirty-seven and twenty-seven, respectively. More famously the deaths of Marilyn Monroe in 1962 and Sylvia Plath in 1963 created, with whatever degree of justification, martyrs, women who were seen to have paid with their lives for exceptional gifts in a society that destroyed them.

While the cult of Plath was literary and limited, Marilyn became an instant emblem on an international scale. Within a year of her death Andy Warhol had made more than twenty silk-screen pictures using her repeated image. She was on Peter Blake and Jann Haworth's cover for the *Sergeant Pepper* album. She was also the semi-autobiographical subject of two of Boty's best-known paintings, *The Only Blonde in the World* (now in the Tate) and *Colour Her Gone*. Boty herself was a remarkably beautiful blonde and like Monroe both sexy and funny. 'I have a – quite a sexual sort of quality but along with a thing that's kind of like, Oh a happy dumb blonde you see,' she told Nell. She too died young, in 1966, the year of Carter's first novel, in which she is glimpsed in the background. 'Colour them gone,' Carter writes of her doomed characters: 'They had fallen through a hole in time into a dimension of pure horror ... colour them all gone.'

Such was the background for all the 'appalling' violence and anger in Carter's work and it may well account for some of it. In her gallery of female archetypes, from Dunbar's golden-haired rude-girls to Marilyn and her myth, the blonde as a type continued to recur as an image of the sado-masochism of sexual relations in contemporary society. Monroe hovers here and there in the early fiction, a 'huge dewy pinup' in a dingy bedsit in *Several Perceptions*, smiling obliviously 'like the Queen of the May' over the damp patches. In *The Sadeian Woman* Carter enrols 'the most famous blonde in the world' into 'the unfortunate sorority of ... Good Bad Girls', of whom Monroe is the cult's 'most notable martyr'. Blondes, she elaborates, have skin of such a delicate texture that they look as if they will bruise at a touch, carrying the exciting stigmata of sexual violence for a long time and that is why gentlemen prefer blondes. Marilyn/Justine has a childlike candour and trust and ... a faint touch of melancholy ... that has been produced by this trust, which is always absolute and always betrayed.

HAIRY FAIRIES:
THE PROSE OF ANGELA CARTER

The 'Japanese Snapshots' of 1971 were apparently the last poems Carter published and they were absorbed into prose in 'A Souvenir of Japan', one of the *Nine Profane Pieces* she published in 1974. In this reminiscence the imagery of the poems develops, like a series of snapshots, to become part of an evocative, ambivalent portrait of Japan. Her time there marked a caesura in her writing, after which came the novels that caused her to be 'ignored'. They are largely ignored here because with hindsight they seem to form a subset, an excursion from the early themes of the poetry to which she returned in her later writing.

Unlike so much that was touted as 'shocking' in the 1960s, *Shadow Dance* (which had its title changed and improved for the paperback to *Honeybuzzard*) still is.

Ghislaine, one of its three protagonists, is another sixties blonde, a 'very young girl' with her 'long, yellow, milkmaid hair and her eyes ... so big and brown ... and her darkened lashes swept down over half her cheeks ... like moonlight on daisies', or at least she was before the story started.

When we meet her she has been slashed with a razor by the man called Honeybuzzard, the charismatic figure at the centre of the story, a dark star around whom events revolve in diminishing circles until the final implosion. Now a scar runs from the corner of Ghislaine's left eyebrow 'down, down, down, down, past nose and mouth and chin until it disappeared below the collar of her shirt'. She is just out of hospital and her wound is still red and purple and raw: 'Even in profile, with the hideous thing turned away, her face was horribly lop-sided, skin, features and all dragged away from the bone.' Thus, in the first three pages, Carter defiles what passes in the book for a heroine. But the shocking thing is that Ghislaine is neither good nor interestingly evil. She is, like the unsatisfactory virgin in 'Unicorn', undistinguished, rather annoying, a bit of a bore, 'rotten, phoney'. She is the sort of girl who 'thought she was shocking people' when 'in fact she was only embarrassing them'. Now, with a face that looks 'half like a baby and half like no face at all', she is doing both.

Carter was never one to stop at embarrassment. The novels of the 1960s, *Shadow Dance*, *The Magic Toyshop*, *Several Perceptions* and *Heroes and Villains*, are among her best work and they spare nobody. Just as Ghislaine is deformed within three pages, so in *The Magic Toyshop* Melanie is brusquely stripped of home, innocence and middle-class comfort by the death of her parents in chapter one. Both novels remain in the penny-plain-and-twopence-coloured world of 'Unicorn', with its cut-out characters. Ghislaine is the fair maid violated, Honeybuzzard a death force in suburban form who, with his pointed, slightly furry ears, has perhaps a forebear in Muriel Spark's Dougal Douglas in *The Ballad of Peckham Rye*: 'one of the wicked spirits that wanders through the world for the ruin of souls' – though the personnel in *Shadow Dance* show little sign of souls. Morris, the final member of the trio, is a bad painter, like William Morris, and similarly surrounded by nineteenth-century bric-a-brac in his nightmarish junk shop. He goes home to his tediously weepy wife, who is called Edna in a nod, perhaps, towards the creator of the 'heart-struck, tearful heroines', while lesser characters have labels more than names, 'little brown Bruno', Henry Glass, whose peace of mind is shattered by Ghislaine, and Emily, with her 'given-gingham-bloody-apron name'.

In her novels Carter's literary heroes have room to stretch their legs. Keats, John Donne, Vaughan and Traherne wander across the back of the stage and occasionally get caught up in the action. *La Belle Dame Sans Merci* echoes through *The Magic Toyshop*, an epigraph from Marvell sets the tone for *Heroes and Villains*. The semi-human creatures of Carroll and Swift with their abrupt changes of scale are translated into characters who are sometimes, like the virgin in 'Unicorn', only a sum of parts. A composite of Mr Rochester's first wife and Miss Havisham drifts through several Carter narratives in the form of an empty wedding dress, usually torn, sometimes on fire. Like Hogarth, she can make 'a scene of furniture' and at times the scenery is more animated than the cast. In *Love* an ex-girlfriend, a studious and respectable person whom the reader never meets, has saturated the flat she left with her unhappiness: 'the tap dripped Annabel's tears and the very sofa seemed re-upholstered with her anguish'.

Shadow Dance is rich in the paraphernalia of England in the mid-sixties, stuck awkwardly between nostalgia and the age of aspiration, of package holidays and wine, usually Mateus Rosé in its ovaloid bottle at the suburban Sunday lunch. The story opens in a pub that is 'an ad-man's crazy dream of a Spanish patio', the pub walls hung with 'unplayable musical instruments and many bull-fight posters, all blood and bulging bulls' testicles and the arrogant yellow satin buttocks of lithe young men ... why then, the horse-brasses, the ship's bell, the fumed oak?'

The urban landscape of the early novels is still scarred by the war. The action is set in the bedsitter hinterland of sad South London or crumbling Bath and Bristol in the clumsily partitioned rooms that could be rented cheaply, 'high in a decaying old house'. Carter is particularly good on depressing bathrooms, the terrifying geysers that thud and judder and then give out a trickle of brown warm water; the pathetic array of toothbrushes, their nakedness standing for the horror of enforced intimacy with strangers. The more flamboyant of her characters, such as Kay in *Several Perceptions*, live in grand ruins, 'a great Georgian palace friable with worm and rot', while the old who have come down in the world in every sense live in basements and ground-floor backs. The past is still close. *The Magic Toyshop* is set in 'a high and windy suburb' which partakes largely of Crystal Palace and while the houses in its 'once stately and solid streets' now 'have the look of queuing for a great knackers' yard', their life in happier days still hangs about them, the 'bustled daughters' of the rising middle classes who

once played parlour ballads on 'rosewood pianos ant-
lered with candlesticks' in 'roast-beef coloured dining
rooms'.

Kay shares a name with the boy in the story of the
Snow Queen and the climate in Carter's novels is
mostly wintery: 'Tea-time on a winter afternoon' she
thought was 'the most British time of the day and
year'. It could be drab, 'weatherless ... sunless, rain-
less, a cool nothing' or ominously beautiful, as in *Love*,
where 'certain yellow, tarnished lights of winter' sig-
nal the onset of psychic terror. It is out of this melan-
choly landscape that pop art and Swinging London
come bursting like weeds on a bomb site, conflating
past and present into the exciting future. Like the Bea-
tles with their *Sergeant Pepper* uniforms, Morris and
Honeybuzzard are discovering Victoriana. In the
underwater light that seeps through the filthy win-
dows of the shop Honeybuzzard, in 'a very white, very
frilly shirt with sleeves as wide as swan's wings', slings
his jacket 'around the pocked shoulders of a green-
stained statue from some abandoned garden, now
probably a housing estate or petrol station'. In its way
it is as much a portrait of an age as Gainsborough's
'Blue Boy'. Breaking into boarded-up houses sched-
uled for demolition, they pick through the old news-
papers, moth-eaten clothes, the detritus of unknown

lives, looking for 'American-bait', '*Observer* design-for-living gear', copper pans, conversation pieces like a genuine oil lamp – 'Polish it up and that's twelve pounds ten'.

Carter's first five novels are dramatisations of states of mind that are made all the more alarming by being tethered so precisely to material reality in time and place. Like 'Unicorn' before them and *The Bloody Chamber* later, they create menace and alienation by contrast with glimpses of impossible safety. Morris's fleeting memory of being 'a snug child in a nursery where red coals glowed behind the disciplined fireguard and the air was sweet with the smell of ironing and bread and milk' is as much a mirage as the good life he imagines his wife leading with another man, in which she would 'bake wholemeal loaves and make chutney from windfall apples and they would go out blackberrying, all the family together, laughing among the red and yellow autumn leaves'. In the event Morris stays miserably with Edna. Honeybuzzard kills Ghislaine in an act of hyperbolic violence. Conventionally, the theory goes, we tell terrifying tales by the fireside so that the warmth and safety of home reduce the monstrous to a pleasurable frisson. In Carter's looking-glass world all is reversed. The firelit circle is the illusion, the reality is darkness and the pathless forest.

After 1971 she disposed of what had been left in her work of 'real' novels. Perhaps her best writing at this time was her journalism and her radio plays, especially *Come Unto These Yellow Sands*, based on the life of the artist and murderer Richard Dadd. Working in a medium where the mind's eye is free to roam but the narrative momentum is still anchored in the chronology of Dadd's unhappy career and startling imagination, the effect is haunting.

Elsewhere in her fiction she was performing something of a high-wire act, risking unintended bathos on one side and forced extravaganza on the other. As she wrote in 'The Loves of Lady Purple', one of the *Nine Profane Pieces*, 'Inside the pink-striped booth of the Asiatic Professor only the marvellous existed and there was no such thing as daylight'. There is often a lack of daylight or narrative air. In another of the stories, 'The Executioner's Beautiful Daughter', set in some crepuscular Central European mountain range, we encounter sadistic voyeurism, murder, an omelette of nearly hatched eggs 'feathered' and 'subtly spiked with claw'. At the end the executioner, still in his leather mask, commits incest with his daughter – on the block. It is hard not to feel it is all a bit overdone. As Francis Wyndham said laconically of this stage in Carter's fiction: 'surely there must be less to life than this'.

The end of another decade marked another turning point in her work. Fittingly for a writer so interested in duality and mirror images, 1979 saw her publish both her most and her least popular books, *The Sadeian Woman* and *The Bloody Chamber*. *The Sadeian Woman* is an extended essay and tends to ramble. Its argument, that Sade liberated women from the concept of sex as merely procreative, never quite coheres but it is full of vivid episodes and images as well as nose tweaking of doctrinaire feminism. It considers Sade from literary and psychoanalytic perspectives and points out that his work has been freely available in only two periods, once during the French Revolution and again in the second half of the twentieth century. Carter draws uncomfortable, sometimes unlikely parallels between the two eras but carries the reader along with her disconcerting briskness and pragmatism. The womb, she writes, is

an organ like any other organ, more useful than the appendix, less useful than the colon but not much use to you at all if you do not wish to utilise its sole function, that of bearing children. At the best of times it is apt to malfunction and cause sickness, pain and inconvenience. The assertion of this elementary fact through the means of a fictional woman involves an entire process of demystification and denial.

Elsewhere she takes up Sade's characters, the virtuous doomed Justine, the vicious triumphant Juliette and the monstrous Durand, like the puppets in *The Magic Toyshop*, and makes them act out the themes that preoccupy her: types, archetypes, the mythical blonde and woman as an assemblage of parts. Juliette is 'Justine-through-the-looking-glass, an inversion of an inversion ... the heroine of a black ... fairy-tale', while Durand is 'the greatest, most monstrous, most potent of all Sade's cruel godmothers. Her habits are those of the wicked stepmother of fairy tale, the ogre queens who devour babies, and her sexual ambivalence is hermaphroditic'. Whatever the essay tells us about Sade, it clearly shows the direction in which Carter was tending. Two years earlier she had translated some of the fairy stories of Charles Perrault. Her version renders his 'elegant witty and sensible pages' into similarly fresh and sympathetic English delightful to read. In the preface she notes that 'each century tends to create or re-create fairy tales after its own taste'. The taste for Perrault's kind of tale had ended abruptly where Sade began, with the French Revolution. Now perhaps was the time to reinvent it once more in the second Sadeian age. In her essay on de la Mare she wrote that 'tales', in the nineteenth-century sense of 'highly structured artefacts with beginnings, middles and ends and a schematic coherence of imagery', were unlike modern short stories. Like William Dunbar, Swift, Sade and Thomas Browne, they offered an alternative to the conventions of contemporary fiction, the sort of thing that might win the Booker Prize, which she characterised as 'a long novel featuring a philosophy don, his mistress and time-travelling to be called *The Owl of Minerva*'.

Thence she came to *The Bloody Chamber*, which was as popular as *The Sadeian Woman* was not, yet it is the other side of exactly the same coin. Both are full of anatomised women, unnatural couplings, death, terror and sado-masochism, but as Carter said of the work of George Macdonald and of Christina Rossetti's *Goblin Market*, 'The latent content diverges so markedly from the superficial text that their self-designation as "fairy tales" seems to function as a screen, or cover, designed to disarm the reader.' The writer in a tale-teller's mask can get away with murder, not to mention many kinds of sex. 'I saw in myself a potential for corruption that took my breath away,' says Bluebeard's bride, who is Justine glimpsing the possibilities of becoming Juliette. 'I longed for him. And he disgusted me.' Like Fevvers in *Nights at the Circus*, Carter saw herself committed to a death-defying act, a storyteller in descent from Scheherazade, 'spinning another story out of the bowels of the last one', because, as she wrote in *Expletives Deleted*, 'the end of all stories, even if the writer forbears to mention it, is death'. She had rarely forborne to mention it, and in *The Bloody Chamber* reddened teeth and claws loom up at every turn. In this, perhaps her best work, it is her easiness with 'once upon a time', in tension with her resistance to 'happy ever after', that lets the fictional argument blossom into startling imagery, while the narrative drives deep into the hairy-fairy underbelly of the nursery. The emotional range is much wider than before. 'Puss in Boots' is comic, 'The Courtship of Mr Lyon' truly poignant, Bluebeard's heroic mother-in-law is entirely admirable and 'The Company of Wolves' has a happy ending of a kind when Red Riding Hood simply gets into bed with the werewolf and is last seen peacefully asleep between his paws.

The 1980s saw Carter's uneven critical fortunes revive with film adaptations of *The Magic Toyshop* and *The Company of Wolves*, for which she wrote the screenplays. It was a decade when monstrous females stalked the land. Diana was the fairy-tale princess going wrong, rampaging over convention, sulking, crying, wreaking havoc and generating mythology on a scale nobody but Carter herself perhaps could have previously imagined. At the same time there was the antitype, 'the visceral anti-Thatcherism' of those years, a violent loathing which Carter shared. It went far beyond politics and turned Britain's first female prime minister into a goggle-eyed spitting image of the wicked witch. Fictional females grew similarly large and strange. In 1983, year of the Tories' landslide victory, on the eve of the miners' strike, Fay Weldon published *Life and Loves of a She-Devil*, with its huge and ugly heroine. The next year saw Carter's *Nights at the Circus*, whose winged protagonist Fevvers is, as Carter emphasises, 'a big girl'.

Carter's last novel was *Wise Children*, which returns to the Brixton of her childhood and to interplay with other authors, including an almost full peal of references to Shakespeare's plays. The writing, she reported, was a struggle and she had a 'deep conviction that when I'd finished something awful would happen'. Within a few pages of the end of the book Dora Chance, one of the twins whose story the novel tells, attempts to break the narrative off short, Scheherazade-like, explaining that much remains unexplained and always must. 'Truthfully,' she tells the reader while the plot is suspended, 'these glorious pauses do, sometimes, occur in the discordant but complementary narratives of our lives and if you choose to stop the story there, at such a pause, and refuse to take it any further, then you can call it a happy ending.' The narrative, however, continues after the pause and the awful thing Carter dreaded had happened by the time *Wise Children* appeared. She was diagnosed with lung cancer and died the following year. 'The fin', as she put it, had 'come rather early' in that siècle, while in the next her reputation goes on to the more enduring kind of fame.

ACKNOWLEDGEMENTS

My principal debt is to Mary-Kay Wilmers, who commissioned the article from which this book grew, who read, commented on and improved the finished text, took time to talk to me about it and mounted a limited defence of the Angry Young Men. Deborah Friedell first suggested I should try to republish *Unicorn*. Susannah Clapp on behalf of the Carter Estate gave permission and Andrew Franklin took the project on for Profile. Steven Dryden and his colleagues at the British Sound Archive enabled me to hear Carter's voice, which I never did in life, and to watch the Omnibus film, *Angela Carter's Curious Room*, shown on BBC2 shortly before her death.

In collecting the poems I was helped by Christopher Reid, who brought several of them to my attention, and Neil Astley of Bloodaxe Books, who once hoped to republish them himself in collaboration with Carter. Her biographer Edmund Gordon explained the mystery of Rankin Crowe. Andrew Motion talked to me about his experience of being Carter's editor, Michael Lee shared his memories of meeting her in the 1980s and Jamie Muir told me about the memorial event held for her at the Brixton Ritzy.

Nell Dunn was generous with her time and her impressions of the situation of women writers in the 1960s, both as it seemed then and in hindsight.

Gavin Stamp, my husband since 2014, is an architectural historian and, like me, a child of the South London suburbs, which I have come to know better and like more in the course of our many long exploratory walks, including an excursion to Angela Carter Close.

BIBLIOGRAPHY

In addition to Angela Carter's own writings I have quoted or extrapolated from the following:

Anne Thorne Architects Partnership, www. annethornearchitects.co.uk

Barker, Paul, 'Angela Carter', *Oxford Dictionary of National Biography*

Calder, John, *The Garden of Eros: The Story of the Paris Expatriates and the Post-War Literary Scene*, 2013

Campbell, James, *Paris Interzone*, 2001

Clapp, Susannah, *A Card from Angela Carter*, 2012

Dundy, Elaine, *The Dud Avocado*, 1958

Dunn, Nell, *Poor Cow*, 1967

   Talking to Women, 1965

Hill, Rosemary, 'Prior Commitment: Aylesford Priory', *Crafts*, September/October 2001, 28–31

Kearney, Patrick J., *The Paris Olympia Press: An Annotated Bibliography*, 1987

Logue, Christopher, *Prince Charming: A Memoir*, 1999

O'Brien, Edna, *Country Girl: A Memoir*, 2012

Ratcliffe, Michael, 'The Angry Young Men', *Oxford Dictionary of National Biography*

Sage, Lorna, *Angela Carter*, 2nd edition, 2007